# $treet $marts

## *for*

# Investor$

## Your Guide to Financial Neighborhoods

# David Wall

To Colleen my wonderful, remarkable,
and adoring wife;

my daughter Alisha, an inspiration to me
and many others;

and my son Nathaniel who makes me
proud and is truly street smart.

I love you guys.

# Contents

Acknowledgements 7

Introduction 9

1. From Beat Cop to Financial Coach:
   To Protect and Serve 13

2. Financial Services Neighborhoods:
   Insurance District 21

3. Financial Services Neighborhoods:
   Brokerville 31

4. Financial Services Neighborhoods:
   RIA Gated Community 39

5. Choosing the Right Advisor:
   Trust but Verify 45

6. Counting the Costs:
   Returns Aren't Everything 51

7. Government and Wall Street:
   Not There for Everyone 61

8. Media and Advertising:
   Selling to Fear and Greed 67

9. Investment Disciplines:
   Portfolio Management 73

10. The Interview:
    Ask the Right Questions 81

Conclusion 89

Glossary 91

# Acknowledgements

I would like to express my deep and sincere thanks to my many friends and staff:

Bruce McNicol, who sent me a crazy text message suggesting I write a book of my stories. Your friendship and wisdom are valued more than you know.

Mike Hamel, my editor, who patiently and skillfully made sense of all my ramblings.

Win Nelson, a truth-teller and good friend who spent countless hours mentoring me in the financial services industry.

James Stocker, who built Microsoft Excel spreadsheets instrumental to making critical portfolio management decisions.

My staff, Barbara Bobbitt, Bill Galgan, Stephen McLeod, Alisha Stocker, Joel Truemper, Nathaniel Wall, and Tabitha Wall, for your loyalty and commitment. Frankly, you make me look better than I deserve.

Finally, to many of my law enforcement friends and colleagues who had my back for so many years.

# Introduction

One lesson I learned about money came from my mom's envelope system. It was her way of budgeting. She had an envelope for groceries, an envelope for entertainment, an envelope for vacations, an envelope for everything. She would always take a little money every pay period and put it in the envelopes. If we wanted to go out for pizza one night, she would check the envelope to see if there was money for that. If there was, we all enjoyed pizza. And if there wasn't, she'd say, "Well, sorry, we'll have to wait until next week." We always made fun of her silly envelope system, but I did learn about budgeting from it.

I knew next to nothing about money when I started on my own. I barely knew what a checking account or a savings account was. And I certainly didn't know anything about stocks or bonds or mutual funds.

Many parents don't teach their kids how to handle money. Few schools have courses on how to understand or budget it. We spend years getting educated for a career to earn money, but aren't given a clue what to do with it once we have it.

All of us are on a financial journey. Whether you are just starting out, are accumulating significant wealth, or are responsible for the oversight of someone else's wealth, there's something in this book for you.

Maybe you simply have questions about the complexities of investing. You're wondering about a 401k, a Roth IRA, an annuity, a mutual fund, an ETF (Exchange Traded Fund), stocks, bonds, private equity, or liquid alternatives.

Maybe you don't know who to trust for sound advice on managing your finances—a successful family member, a broker, an insurance agent, or an independent investment advisor.

Maybe you have been burned by a financial advisor who has not served you well or who has mismanaged your money or perhaps stolen from you.

Maybe you are thinking about retirement and need professional help in managing your savings so they last as long as you do.

Maybe you are retired and aren't sure how to make the most of your retirement nest egg.

Maybe you are planning for the final distribution of your estate to your heirs.

Wherever you are on your financial journey, it's safe to say all investors want two things: 1) a basic understanding of things beyond our experience, training and control; and 2) a prudent way to accumulate wealth for ourselves or those who have entrusted us with their wealth. I believe I can help you with both of these based on my more than thirty years of observations and experiences in the financial services industry and more than twenty years as a policeman and detective. I've gone from beat cop, to detective, to CEO of a wealth planning and asset management advisory firm overseeing more than $1.3 billion in assets.

The investigative skills I developed as a detective, along with the formal education and certifications I picked up during more than thirty years of investment experience, have prepared me for the sometimes brutal financial services industry. In the following pages, I'll share my hard-won insights, successes, and failures from my own financial journey to help you better navigate yours. I'll introduce you to the concept of a fiduciary and explain why you need to work with one. And I'll tell you who else needs to be on your financial team.

This book is not a step-by-step financial planning or wealth management guide. It's a practical, understandable training course on how to avoid some of the pitfalls in investing and identify smart, ethical, and trustworthy advisors who can help you accomplish your goals.

David Wall

# 1

# From Beat Cop to Financial Coach
# To Protect and Serve

How many people would stick with a new job if, four days into it, they got shot in the face?

I did.

For twenty-one years.

My name is Dave Wall and this is my story.

I was born in the Chicagoland area, Elmhurst, in 1954, the oldest of three children. My dad was a carpenter. My mom was a stay-at-home mom. My childhood was pretty normal. I was an average student in high school, ran some cross country, and played some basketball. When I graduated in 1972, I went to a local community college. That's where I became interested in police science. It happened by accident. I came across a brochure for police science and thought, *Hey, what the heck. I can give this a whirl.*

Following this lead I attended the College of DuPage for two years, where I attended police science classes. While in school, I also got a part-time position as a cadet with the Addison Police Department, working as a dispatcher. After college, I moved on to a full-time position in Rolling Meadows where I dispatched for the police and fire departments. Eventually, I was selected to supervise the communications division. I then began testing to get a position as a full-time police officer. On September 28, 1978, I was hired as a police officer in Addison. I was sworn in on a Wednesday evening and promptly got myself shot on Sunday, October 1, my fourth day on the job.

I was with my field training officer. We responded to a "man with a gun" call and the information from dispatch was correct. A man with a shotgun came out the front door of a residence and fired, spraying the squad with birdshot. Several pellets ricocheted off the front of the squad car and struck me in the face. The next thing I remember was being treated by an off-duty Addison firefighter-paramedic. From there it was off to the hospital where I was admitted and subsequently had a little plastic surgery to remove the pellets from my face. Today, if I am asked, "How come you're so ugly?" I say, "Because I got shot in the face. What's your excuse?"

If you're wondering what happened to the gunman, he was shot three times by other officers. Paramedics saved his life. He was later found guilty of armed violence and aggravated battery, and sentenced to ten years in prison. In retrospect, I believe the incident was what's known as suicide by cop. When the guy did his required time and was released, he took his own life.

After the shooting, I never questioned law enforcement as a career. My wife was supportive and didn't ask me to quit. Colleen and I met at church years earlier and were married in 1976. I finished my basic training and picked up additional training. I went to accident investigation school and did a lot of traffic enforcement for about six years.

Then in my sixth year, I was assigned to investigations. Being a detective wasn't a promotion; it was an assignment. It took me off the midnight shift, which was nice. I now had a lot of flexibility in my schedule. It was supposed to be a two-year assignment, but I spent the next fifteen years as a detective.

We investigated everything: homicides, rapes, auto thefts, financial crimes, and property crimes. We were a small department, so we had to be somewhat familiar with everything. As time went on, however, we became more specialized. I ended up becoming the financial crimes investigator. I investigated a lot of frauds, forgeries, embezzlements—that sort of stuff.

## Financial Services

This isn't what started my interest in financial services, though. That came through my insurance agent. He sold me insurance and annuities and taught me about the time value of money and how money grows. That stirred my interest in the topic. I was persuaded to sell life insurance and annuities and got an insurance license to sell those products. Life insurance and annuities were the answer to everything. I was discouraged by my supervisor from asking about other financial options like mutual funds.

While assigned to the patrol division and working different shifts, I studied for a securities license called a series 6. The exam is a license that allows an advisor to sell mutual funds. I passed the exam while working part-time with a company called Waddell & Reed. But the problem I saw with Waddell & Reed was they were largely captive. This meant I was only encouraged to sell their family of mutual funds that paid a healthy commission. This was back in the late 1980s when mutual funds were very expensive.

I continued to work the cop job and pursue more education in the financial services industry by pursuing a Certified Financial Planner (CFP®) designation. This training took two years and I completed the program in 1990. The financial services business was a good diversion from my cop job. Police work can make a person cynical. When first starting the job, rookies want to save the world and really help people. It only takes a few years before they realize they're not going to save the world. They're making a difference. They do things that matter, but they don't make the difference they expected.

In May 1990, I started a business and registered as a fee-only investment advisor with the Securities and Exchange

Commission. Colleen and I worked together in our basement. I clearly remember putting in a phone that was going to cost me $25 a month. I didn't know where I was going to get the money to pay the bill. Today, I wish my phone bill was only twenty-five bucks!

In 1991, there was a vacant trustee position on our local pension board. My colleagues at the police department knew I'd completed my CFP® studies. They trusted that I was up for the job. I was elected and continued to serve on the board for about ten years.

I continued with my education at the Wharton School of Business and received the Certified Investment Management Analyst (CIMA®) certification in 1995. This training gave me a solid foundation for institutional consulting and some formal education in the area.

I became more familiar with the institutional marketplace and began to see the abuses going on there. The brokerage community had their hands firmly around the necks of the pension trustees who were paying way too much for what they were getting. There were some very unsophisticated investors who were responsible for a lot of money. I'm reminded of a story about the broker who bragged he had the best clients in the world: "Stupid ones with a lot of money."

In 1998, a statute changed, which really expanded the investment landscape for Illinois public funds. That's when my business really started to pop because now the pension boards were able to utilize more investment tools and products. Since I wore a police uniform, I had credibility with my peers. I just had to demonstrate that I knew something about investment portfolios.

I was still a full-time detective, but I was getting tired of the lying, the cheating, the stealing. The two careers were taking a toll at work and at home. I was losing my patience with people. My blood pressure was through the roof.

I always thought I would work the cop job until I was fifty, when my pension would kick in. But as the business became successful, it got to the point where I couldn't do both well. Police work is a young man's job. Don't misunderstand me—it was fun much of the time, but also sad at times. My cynical joke was, "I have the best job in the world. I go to work every day and all I deal with are sex and violence."

But it became less and less fun and I just got tired of people lying to me all the time. A good friend of mine told me, "Dave, I think it's time. You need to pull the pin and go."

So at the ripe old age of forty-six, I made the decision to retire from the police department on January 1, 2000. I had put in twenty-one years but couldn't start to draw my pension until I was fifty, so I went into the financial services business full-time.

The business continued to grow and I was getting some of my continuing education requirements at an investment conference in Naples, Florida. That is where I met Win Nelson. It must have been a divine act. We were unexpectedly put together on a golf cart. Win became a friend and tremendous mentor. He spent hours on the phone helping me hone my skills in asset allocation, portfolio construction, and asset management. I am eternally grateful for his friendship and coaching.

## Protecting and Coaching

The question I am asked most often is how I went from police detective to financial advisor. These are two very different occupations with very different educational requirements. They don't seem to connect, but I actually think they do. Both occupations have elements of fairness, justice, and empathy.

Most people in police work choose that career because they want to help protect those who may not be able to protect themselves. Cops protect the public by investigating and enforcement. Financial coaches protect the investor by teaching and transparency.

For me, it's about protecting people. In both fields, I had the opportunity to do that. My motivation in both settings can be summarized in two words: *protection* and *fairness*. As a detective, it was about protecting the public and ensuring fairness under the law. It's the same thing in the investment world, where the investor is the public.

> **That's one of the characteristics of a good advisor; he or she is also a teacher/coach.**

When I moved over into the institutional investment world, I found some brokers who were just pillaging pension funds because their clients were often uneducated and uninformed. It wasn't their field of expertise. I wanted to protect investors from brokers who were only in it for the money.

Part of protecting investors and ensuring fairness involves educating and coaching them. That's one of the characteristics of a good advisor; he or she is also a teacher/coach. The popular author and financial advisor Dave Ramsey talks about having the heart of a teacher, not a salesman. A teacher/coach is interested in you; a salesman is interested in your pocketbook.

That's one of the ways you can evaluate advisors. Are they teachers? Do they educate you and help you understand? If they can't clearly communicate their investment strategy in a manner that you can understand, why should you trust them? As an investor, you must learn to determine who's just selling you something, who's authentic, and who has your best interest at heart. You do this by learning to ask the right questions to identify the smart, ethical advisor.

In "The Interview" chapter, you'll find a list of such questions. But for now, let's take a look at the neighborhoods where these advisors hang out.

## TAKEAWAYS

- Financial coaches protect the investor by teaching and transparency.
- A teacher/coach is interested in you; a salesman is interested in your pocketbook.
- You learn who's authentic and has your best interest at heart by asking the right questions.

# 2

# Financial Services Neighborhoods Insurance District

Policework took me into some very crime-ridden places. As a detective, I recall ending up in some very unsafe neighborhoods. So unsafe that moms put their babies and young children to sleep in bathtubs to protect them from possible stray gunfire. Other neighborhoods experienced modest crime while still others were very safe, such as gated communities with a security guard at the entrance and sophisticated alarm systems in the homes.

There are different neighborhoods in the financial services industry as well. Some are dangerous to your financial health; others are very safe. Here's how I categorize the financial services neighborhoods:

- The least safe neighborhood is the insurance district.
- A safer neighborhood, but not all that safe, is Brokerville.
- The safest neighborhood is the registered investment advisor (RIA) gated community.

I use the following criteria to rate the types of advisors you will run into in these neighborhoods:

- What emotion is the advisor selling to? For example, is it fear or greed, or are they educating and coaching?
- Is the advisor selling a product or selling a service?
- What regulatory oversight is in place for the advisor?

• Is the advisor objective, disclosing all potential conflicts of interests?
• How is the advisor paid?
• Does the advisor acknowledge in writing that he or she is a fiduciary?

A fiduciary is a person (or organization) that acts on behalf of another person to manage assets. A fiduciary is legally bound to act in the other's best interests. When choosing to work with an advisor you should insist that they are a fiduciary.

The typical way to get introduced to these neighborhoods is a solicited or unsolicited referral:

"My golf buddy Rich told me about this insurance guy he uses."

"My brother-in-law has an account with this brokerage firm that he likes."

Or you'll see some advertisement on TV that sounds too good to be true. It probably is.

Or you'll walk into your bank and across the lobby there's a well-dressed young person ready to sell you their proprietary product, for a healthy commission of course.

In this chapter we'll look at the insurance district. The broker neighborhood and registered investment advisor neighborhood will be discussed in the next chapters.

## One Industry, Two Streets

In the insurance district, you will encounter two kinds of residents or agents. There are those who recommend insurance coverage to protect against catastrophic losses. Some examples are automobile policies to cover accidents or theft, homeowners' policies to cover a fire or burglary, and life insurance in the event of the unexpected death of a key provider in a family. Home and auto policies are commonly referred to as property and casualty.

These insurance agents usually are also licensed to sell life insurance and annuities but often refrain from doing so, with exception of term life insurance. They take a holistic view of an individual's financial wellness and may suggest you seek out a financial planner or wealth manager for planning and investment advice.

Andy, a trusted friend and successful insurance agent who focuses on such coverages, puts it this way, "The insurance agent plays defense and the financial planner plays offense. Offense is more glamorous, but defense wins games."

An agent who recommends appropriate coverages and monitors coverages with timely recommended changes is critical and needs to be part of your financial wellness team.

The other resident in the insurance district, and who frankly causes me a little heartburn, is the insurance advisor who provides financial planning and wealth management advice. It seems their solution in every situation is cash-value life insurance and annuities.

## Life Insurance and Annuities

Universal life and whole life are two types of cash-value life insurance policies. They provide a certain amount of death benefit, build cash value, and are often recommended to be permanent coverage for the insured's lifetime. They are often sold with the caveat that the premiums are flexible. Part of each premium pays the mortality and administrative costs of the policy; the rest goes into an account that earns some rate of return. Term insurance, on the other hand, is a policy that does not build cash value and only pays when the insured dies. Death benefits paid to the beneficiary are income tax free.

The purpose of any life insurance policy is to protect assets, most likely the future earnings of the family member who's providing financial support for the family. Problem is, you need lots of coverage when you're young and must provide for your family in the event of premature death. Policies that build cash value are likely to leave you woefully short on coverage and are very expensive. An appropriate coverage is necessary and should be at least ten times your current income. A person making $50,000 a year should have at least $500,000 in death benefit coverage.

Don't count any coverage your employer may provide after determining your needs. If you lose your job, you will likely lose your coverage. A second risk is that you may no longer be insurable when you lose the job. I recommend purchasing an inexpensive term policy to get all the coverage you need.

An annuity is a financial contract with an insurance company in which a person makes a lump-sum payment or series of payments. In return, the person receives regular disbursements, beginning either immediately or at some future date. There are many types but the most common are fixed annuities or variable annuities.

A fixed annuity pays a fixed rate of interest that can change from time to time, usually on the policy anniversary. A variable annuity provides a menu of investment options similar to mutual funds that invest in stocks or bonds. These are commonly called subaccounts. Annuities enjoy the benefit of tax deferral on any earnings or appreciation until funds are withdrawn from the contract.

## Cashing Out Insurance Products

Both cash value life insurance policies and annuities are generally recommended because tax is deferred on any earnings to a future day. This allows your savings to grow faster. Funds accumulated in an annuity can be withdrawn by surrendering the contract and taking a lump sum or by taking regular monthly payments over some period of time.

Keep in mind annuities are subject to 10 percent penalties if cash is taken out before age 59½. This is a real liquidity problem if you are young. Distributions from cash value life insurance policies can be taken before age 59 ½ and are often sold as tax free. This is because distributions requested by the owner of the contract are considered to be loans.

Sounds good, but as you get older the cost for the coverage keeps going up. If the cash in the policy is not sufficient to cover the costs of the insurance, then you must make additional premium payments, if payments had been stopped. So when you are older and no longer feel you need the coverage and do not want to pay additional premiums, you may decide to surrender the policy to get whatever cash is left. This can result in meaningful tax consequences if over time you've taken loans against the policy.

I have a client who for many years made payments to a universal life policy. It was sold to him as a liquid investment paying 4 percent. Anytime he wanted money he could take a loan against the cash value of the policy and would not owe any tax. Great idea, until he reached his 70s and was told he needed to add additional funds to his policy because there wasn't enough cash in the policy to cover the death benefit. Recognizing he no longer needed the coverage, he surrendered the policy. The tax consequences to that transaction were significant, about $10,000. Why the tax? The loans he'd taken over the years were now characterized as income and thus taxable!

So much for permanent tax-free, cash-value life insurance policies.

## Selling to Fear

A client once told me of his experience with an insurance advisor. The advisor's message was always, "The stock market is overcooked; the next crash is coming soon. The sky is dark, threatening, and going to fall. The world is coming to an end. The markets are fraught with risk and you must protect your initial investment at all costs. So invest and save in annuities."

There are two things that must occur to avoid losing your initial investment in a traditional annuity, assuming there are no riders attached to the contract. Riders are expensive and increase costs, resulting in lower returns. First, the value of the annuity must be less than what you originally invested. Second, the owner must die. Seems like the outcome is not so good for the owner but it's great for the beneficiaries.

> ## What was the likelihood of losing money in the stock market over a seven year period? Less than 2 percent.

Annuities can serve a purpose, but I think they are not appropriate in the accumulation season of your financial journey. They may, and I emphasize *may*, be appropriate when an individual cannot, due to their financial circumstances, or will not take risks in the market and desires a guaranteed income in retirement. This is likely the result of failing to properly plan for retirement.

Now, no one likes to lose money, but the fears described above aren't realistic. Consider this illustration. Annuities typically have a seven-year surrender charge. That means if you surrender the contract and ask for your money in the early years of the contract the insurance company charges you a penalty. By the way, you may also owe taxes if you surrender the contract before age 59½.

I ran the historical rolling monthly seven-year returns, a common time period when surrender charges apply to an annuity contract, of the Standard and Poor 500 index (S&P 500). The S&P 500 consists of 500 of the largest US companies traded on US exchanges. The analysis covered a 50-year period from January 1970 to January 2020.

What was the likelihood of losing money in the stock market over a seven year period? Less than 2 percent. That's right. You had a 98 percent likelihood of a positive outcome in any given seven years. The worst seven-year period was negative 2.6 percent and the best seven-year period was positive 21.8 percent. So, you see these fears are not realistic, especially while accumulating savings.

If I gave you $1000 and the choice of putting the money in your pocket or into a slot machine with a 98 percent chance of a payoff, which would you choose? I suspect the slot machine.

So much for the world coming to an end. Believe in America, invest in American companies, and be patient.

The insurance advisor is selling to fear when he pushes annuities by stressing you can never lose your principal. You won't lose your principal, but returns will suffer. He might imply his services are free. He won't use the word "commission" but rather explains that companies pay him a "finder's fee." Folks, that's code for commissions.

One of the greatest abuses I have repeatedly seen in the insurance industry is utilizing annuities to fund individual retirement accounts (IRAs). This includes both traditional and Roth IRAs. These products do not serve the investor well during the accumulation season of their financial journey. They are expensive, have limited investment options, and contain contract language severely limiting liquidity.

A better alternative would be to open an IRA account with a firm like Schwab, Vanguard, or Fidelity and to diversify the portfolio across several asset classes. You can read more about that in chapter nine. Help from a competent advisor would be beneficial here.

### Regulatory Oversight

Regulatory oversight in this neighborhood is weak and often more reactive to a complaint rather than proactive. The following story shows the danger of poor regulatory oversight in this part of town. It concerns Ronald Morley, who is based in Maryland. In 2006, Morley's home state barred him from selling securities because he indicated to investors that certain investments were safe, even though state regulators had ruled otherwise.

The Securities and Exchange Commission (SEC) is the federal government agency responsible for protecting investors. In 2016 they barred Morley from working as a broker or at a registered investment advisory firm. He had convinced 130 clients to invest in a fraudulent stock offering called Summit Trust Company that earned him more than $3 million in commissions. Morley was convicted of securities fraud in Kansas in a case that cited $800,000 in losses suffered by four investors. He was given thirty-six months probation.

Despite these criminal activities, Morley is still licensed to sell insurance in Maryland (although he's banned from selling securities there). The fact that salespeople have been barred by one state regulator but can continue to get a green light from other state regulators is confounding.

## Questions

Let's run through some of the questions I listed at the beginning of this chapter:

- What emotion is the advisor selling to? Insurance advisors often sell to unrealistic fear.
- Is the advisor selling a product or selling a service? Insurance advisors tend to recommend products with a limited choice of investment options.
- What regulatory oversight is in place for the advisor? Limited, virtually none.
- How is the advisor paid? Insurance advisors are paid on commissions, which creates a potential conflict of interest.
- Does the advisor acknowledge in writing that he or she is a fiduciary? Insurance advisors are not fiduciaries. They do not have a management agreement with the client.

For the reasons touched on above, I rate the financial advisor insurance district as an unsafe neighborhood. The next, somewhat safer neighborhood the everyday investor may probably explore is a place I call Brokerville.

## TAKEAWAYS

- Some neighborhoods are dangerous to your financial health; others are very safe.
- The likelihood of losing money in the stock market over a seven-year period is less than 2 percent.
- Regulatory oversight is weak with regard to insurance advisors, often more reactive to a complaint than proactive.

# 3

# Financial Services Neighborhoods
# Brokerville

B rokerville has two districts. Depending on which area you wander into, you'll find different brokers working in each.

### Warehouse District

The first section of Brokerville is the warehouse district. Businesses here are like Home Depot, where you go when you're building or repairing your house and need some materials and tools. The firms here are commonly referred to as discount brokers. Companies like Charles Schwab and E-Trade got their start providing this kind of service. They were a lower-cost alternative to the big brokerage firms and did not tell investors what stocks to buy or sell.

At Home Depot, you walk in and tell the associate you want to buy a hammer, some nails, and eight sheets of plywood. The associate tells you where you can find those items and then meets you at the register where you pay for what you selected. Like the Home Depot associate, the discount broker is merely providing or "stocking the shelves" with lots of securities products. You choose which securities you want to purchase and they provide the platform to execute the trade and then settle the trade in your account. They do not give financial planning or asset management advice.

The discount broker is just giving you the tools to manage

your own portfolio. Their fees are all pretty much the same. These brokers are not allowed to call themselves advisors, just like the Home Depot associates don't represent themselves as licensed contractors. The broker representative will generally get paid a salary just like the associate at Home Depot.

The investors who shop here are the do-it-yourselfers. They're not hiring a financial professional; they just need a broker to help them do what they want to do. Discount brokers can provide that service at a lower cost. You may not meet these brokers face to face. You can place your order by phone or go online. You don't have to talk to the broker at all.

### Full-Service Brokerage Houses: The High-Rent District

On May 1, 1975, the stock market changed forever. From this date on, brokerage companies were allowed to charge varying commission rates. Prior to this, all brokerage firms charged the same price for stock trades. This was the first time in 180 years that trading fees would be set by market competition instead of a fixed price.

> They are salespeople and only required to ensure the transactions they are executing are "suitable" for their customers.

Traditional brokers recognized their services were becoming obsolete and they needed to become more competitive. They had to find some rationale to justify their higher fees and to stay in business, so they started calling themselves financial advisors or financial consultants. They work in well-known firms like Edward Jones, Morgan Stanley, and Wells Fargo Advisors. They are salespeople and only required to ensure the transactions they are executing are "suitable" for their customers.

These brokers couldn't sell something to someone unless

it was suitable. The idea was to prevent them from selling junk bonds to eighty-year-old-ladies. This wasn't a very high threshold, though, because brokers could sell clients a suitable security that paid a 1 percent commission or the same security that paid a 5 percent commission.

The suitability standard was never seen as particularly good. Clients were paying way too much and brokers were getting rich. Their clients weren't necessarily successful; some of them were left in a deep financial hole.

However, the SEC is tasked with trying to protect the unwary. They want the everyday investor to understand the difference between a broker (salesperson) and an investment advisor. The SEC made a rule prohibiting these brokers from calling themselves "advisors" unless they acknowledged they were a fiduciary and subjected themselves to the rules and responsibilities that apply to fiduciaries.

The brokerage community objected and challenged these rules in court. Unfortunately, they prevailed, so the SEC went back to the drawing board. The result was a new rule commonly called the "best interest rule." Under this rule, brokers can't recommend a security or a product unless they've determined it's in the best interest of their client and provided some additional disclosure.

The problem is that this standard is no different than the "suitability" standard. Nothing really changed; it was just putting lipstick on a pig. In fact, things got more confusing. As it turns out, the SEC's rule does not level the playing field. It does not create a uniform standard requiring brokers to be fiduciaries like a registered investment advisor. Instead it only partially raises the conduct standards for brokers, with a new "regulation best interest" requirement. It obligates them to act in the best interests of their clients when making investment recommendations.

THESE NEW REGULATIONS WILL COMPLETELY
CHANGE HOW WE GET AROUND THEM, SIR.

To help further clarify the nature of the relationship between customers and their brokers and investment advisors, the SEC established a new disclosure form. Form CRS (short for customer/client relationship summary) provides a "simple, plain language" four-page explanation of the consumer's relationship with the broker or advisor.

The SEC is at least attempting to raise the standards for brokers, with an aim to further clarify the nature of the brokers' relationship with customers and how it differs from the registered investment advisors' relationship with clients. Yet at the same time, introducing a "regulation best interest" requirement has only created more confusion. The "interests" standard for brokers and a "fiduciary" standard for registered investment advisors (RIAs) are not created equal.

This raises the question of whether it's finally time for title reform by proposing that brokers will no longer be permitted to use any title that contains the word "advisor." But for now, they can make such a representation because their employer is dually registered as a broker and a registered investment advisor. How do you know which hat the traditional broker is wearing? Simple. Ask one question: Are you willing to acknowledge in writing you are acting as a fiduciary in your advisory capacity?

So in the end, traditional brokers can still make money by selling products that pay healthy commissions. The brokerage house will have a list of recommended securities the broker can sell from. They're likely to recommend the products that are going to make them, or the brokerage house, the most money—for example, wrap accounts where clients pay fees as high as 3 percent of the account value annually. In effect these brokers are salespeople and it's buyer beware!

Let me say a word about brands. We've all heard of Charles Schwab, Raymond James, Edward Jones, Wells Fargo, and Morgan Stanley. These are well-known firms with name recognition and deep resources. But the brokers in these houses aren't any smarter than the independent advisors in smaller companies. The licensing requirements and regulatory exams are the same to work in either neighborhood. The same kinds of financial products are available in both places but the independent advisor is likely to be a whole lot more objective. He is also likely to have a lower overhead. Who do you think pays for all those TV ads and offices filled with marble, mahogany furniture, and expensive artwork? The clients.

I will close this chapter with a broker story from a public pension fund client. The client was working with an Edward Jones broker who recommended and purchased certain mutual funds that were subject to surrender charges or penalties. While the broker was meeting with the client and me, I asked that important question, "Are you a fiduciary to the plan?"

"No," he said.

I then asked, "Could you enter into an agreement with the board where you acknowledged you are a fiduciary?"

'Yes."

"Great," I said. "Would you continue to hold the same funds in that case?"

He answered, "No, the holdings in the account would likely be very different."

Recommending funds with commissions obviously influenced his objectivity. He was not acting as a fiduciary. Fiduciaries are held to a higher standard, which is why I believe you should only work with an advisor who is also a fiduciary.

Some people think I'm cynical. I prefer to think of myself as skeptical. I'm a realist. I assume people are going to do what's in their own best interest.

Many brokers are sales representatives who disguise themselves as financial advisors. Let's use the questions from the insurance chapter (pages 28, 29) to grade the brokers:

- What emotion is the broker selling to? Brokers often sell to greed.
- Is the broker selling a product or a service? Products. Brokers tend to recommend products such as mutual funds that carry heavy costs.
- What regulatory oversight is in place for the broker? Some oversight by the firm and SEC.
- How is the broker paid? Brokers get paid healthy commissions, which creates a potential conflict of interest.
- Does the broker acknowledge in writing he or she is a fiduciary? No. Brokers do not have management agreements with clients and they will not act as fiduciaries.

I would rate Brokerville as safer than the insurance district, but not as secure as the registered investment advisor community we'll visit next.

## TAKEAWAYS

- Discount brokers give you the tools to manage your own portfolio. Their fees are all pretty much the same.
- The new "best interest" standard does little to improve the old "suitability" standard, allowing brokers to continue to use the terms "advisor" or "consultant."
- Always ask brokers to acknowledge whether or not they are fiduciaries.

# 4

# Financial Services Neighborhoods
# RIA Gated Community

This neighborhood is the equivalent of a gated community. The houses are well maintained. The streets are safe. This is the home of registered investment advisors. They are typically more transparent than other advisors. They acknowledge right from the start that they are fiduciaries.

If you want to be trading stocks yourself, you need to go a discount broker, not a registered investment advisor (RIA). But if you want a comprehensive plan based on your specific financial situation and long term goals, you need an investment professional.

Registered investment advisors sell services such as financial planning and wealth management. They work with clients to give them a tailored plan that may include maximizing their Social Security benefits or Medicare, or guiding them in tax planning.

## Team Effort

Registered investment advisors are like general practitioners in the medical field. They know enough about a wide range of things to be able to give sound advice. They can recognize when something may be wrong and steer clients toward good financial health. As full service advisors, they care for a client's financial life the way doctors care for physical life.

Suppose you go to your doctor for a regular checkup, and

he discovers an irregular heartbeat. You will most likely get a referral to see a cardiologist. In a similar way, when financial advisors recognize issues outside of their area of expertise, they will refer you to other experts like estate-planning attorneys or tax specialists.

Most advisors are not attorneys or tax specialists. If they are, great. If not, you need to add two more professionals to your team. You need a knowledgeable estate-planning attorney to put together legal documents allowing you to pass your wealth on to the next generation. How investment accounts are set up—for example joint tenancy with right of survivorship, or transfer on death—can accomplish the transfer of wealth to your heirs. But these don't address other issues that may pop up—for example, challenges from a former spouse or an unhappy family member. An estate attorney can mitigate these kinds of challenges.

Everyone's circumstances and wishes are different. Some may need a sophisticated trust, others only a simple will. If you don't have a will, the state has one for you. It's called probate. It's expensive and won't do what you had in mind.

You will also need a durable power of attorney. This document allows a trusted person to manage your financial affairs if you are unable to. A power of attorney for healthcare is also needed. This legal document allows you to designate another person to make medical decisions for you if you cannot.

A word of warning here. Use a qualified and experienced estate attorney. I recommend not using online services such as LegalZoom, LegalShield, or Rocket Lawyer. I had a family member who decided to take a shortcut and did not consult an attorney when making a change to her will. Upon her death it was learned certain documents were not properly witnessed. As a result, her final wishes were not fulfilled.

Your circumstances may also require the services of a sharp accountant or CPA to make sure that when you pay your taxes you retain as much money as you are legally entitled to. The financial advisor and these three professionals—a competent property and casualty insurance agent, an estate attorney, and a tax specialist—round out your financial wellness team. Utilizing the services of these professionals goes a long way to ensuring success on your financial journey.

## Key Difference

A helpful distinction to make among the insurance advisor, broker advisor, and registered investment advisor is identifying what services they are offering and how they get paid. These two criteria have a profound effect on their objectivity. Insurance advisors are largely captive to the insurance industry and in many cases held captive to a specific carrier. They are also paid with commissions.

Broker-advisors who are not fiduciaries may or may not be captive to one family of funds, but they can also run afoul with proprietary products offered by their firms. Registered investment advisors give advice and counsel. They are not beholden to a specific investment product and are only paid the fee agreed to by the client. The following analogy may give better insight into these issues.

Take car dealers as a good way to understand captive agents and fee-only advisors. A Chevy dealer can only sell Chevys. The Chevy salesperson gets a commission on what he sells, so it's in his best interest to sell you the most expensive Chevy. He may know there are cars that are similar and may be less expensive or have extra bells and whistles. Frankly, other makes of cars may be a better value. He may own one of these vehicles, but he is not likely to send you to a dealer that sells that car.

CarMax, on the other hand, sells any kind of car you might want. CarMax offers all makes and models and price ranges. Their sales staff are salaried and aren't paid commissions. They have no more incentive to sell you a BMW than a Chevy.

They just want to know what kind of vehicle you're looking for. Their motivation is a satisfied customer. They are like fee-only advisors.

While both salespeople are selling cars, the Chevy sales staff has to focus on selling products because they're paid on commission. Sales is the driver in their business. The CarMax sales staff can focus on service because they're paid a salary. Service is the focus of their business.

Captive agents are limited in the products they can sell and the financial tools in their toolbox. They may have a conflict between selling what pays the highest commissions and doing what's in their clients' best interests. Fee-only advisors can be more objective in putting the client's interests first because they are paid a set fee and aren't motivated by commissions.

## An advisor is, in the end, a salesperson. But is he selling products or services?

Let's use another illustration to show how a fee-only agent can be more objective in putting the client's interests first. Say you go to Home Depot to buy an appliance. They have GE, they have Whirlpool, and they have different price ranges. The salesman helping you doesn't care if you buy a GE or a Whirlpool. His job is to be a good advisor. This starts with finding out what you need and want. He might ask, "How big a refrigerator do you need? Do you want the freezer on the side or bottom? How much do you want to spend?"

If you're like me, you want a salesperson who knows the details about the various products—information that I don't know but should have, before I make a decision. I also really like it when I find someone who can speak from personal experience or is passionate about helping me get the best deal. He may be indifferent to what I actually buy, but he wants to be of service.

## Products or Services?

An advisor is, in the end, a salesperson. But is he selling products or services? If he's incentivized by commissions, this tends to distort his objectivity. If he's not objective, then he's not doing what's in the client's best interest?

A registered advisor will charge a reasonable fee. Now, there are no businesses without some conflicts of interest. When the brokerage houses set up their menus of what their brokers can sell, they have a huge conflict between their profits and the client's best interests. But it's different with registered investment advisors because they are fiduciaries who work for a set dollar amount or a percentage of the client's portfolio. The range of fees are typically annual fees of 1 to 1.5 percent. But I have seen fee schedules as high as 2.5 percent.

When the value of a client's portfolio goes up, the advisor does well. When the value of a client's portfolio goes down the advisor also suffers. Their interests are aligned, as opposed to the brokerage houses, which are not necessarily aligned because their revenues are driven by selling expensive products.

Hopefully, I have given you a better understanding of the financial services neighborhoods and the advisors who work there. In the interview chapter, I'll share specific questions to ask these advisors, and the reasonable answers you should expect to hear.

Back to our checklist (pages 28, 29) to rate this community. Registered investment advisors (RIAs) sell a service. They have a clearly defined approach to managing a client's personal wealth. They get paid a fee, not commissions. They are not captive in recommending products. This eliminates most conflicts of interest.

RIAs must have a management agreement with clients and act as fiduciaries. They have good regulatory oversight by retaining specialized compliance personnel who monitor them, and they are subject to SEC audits from time to time.

They also network with other professionals to build a solid team built for defense and offense. These are the reasons the RIA community is by far the safest place to find an advisor who's right for you.

## TAKEAWAYS

- Registered investment advisors acknowledge right from the start that they are fiduciaries.
- Fee-only advisors can be more objective in putting the client's interests first because they are paid a set fee and aren't motivated by commissions.
- Develop an experienced team of professionals that includes an independent financial advisor, a property and casualty insurance agent, an estate attorney, and a tax specialist.

# 5

## Choosing the Right Advisor
## Trust but Verify

Trustworthy advisors aren't selling returns or high commission products. They are fiduciaries selling a service for a fee. They are financial life coaches. They talk about things like what happens if your spouse predeceases you. Or they know you have a special needs child who needs full-time care and address how to handle that.

One of my first personal wealth clients was retiring from AT&T. He was getting a lump sum and wanted help managing it. He later told me why he hired me.

"Dave, you were the only guy who didn't talk about investment returns. You talked about planning our lives and making our money last. Everybody else wanted just to focus on the returns."

Perhaps you want to begin working with an advisor for the first time or have been working with someone and want to explore other options. Maybe, after learning about the advisors who frequent these different neighborhoods, it's time for a checkup.

As we've seen by touring the various financial neighborhoods, advisors may be motivated by different criteria. It may be the size of your account or the method by which they are compensated. Or maybe they are captive and less objective. The advisor you want is the one who is authentic, smart, and trustworthy. You need to be street smart about whom to trust to help shape your financial future.

So where do you start if you are looking for an advisor? When I've asked my friends what they would do if they were looking for help with financial planning or wealth management, every single time they responded, "I'd ask a trusted family member or friend for a referral."

A huge word of caution here. You might have a family member, good friend, or somebody from your church who works in one of these financial services neighborhoods. Despite the relationship, you need to do some investigation on these people. They have to be able to answer the tough questions you would ask any advisor. They shouldn't get a free pass just because they share the same heritage or go to the same church. This may be an excellent starting point. But it begs the question of how much due diligence that family member or friend did on their advisor. How did they find that advisor? In what neighborhood does the advisor reside?

## Misplaced Trust

Just one story about a so-called "advisor" who was managing money for family and several colleagues at work. This individual was also an associate pastor at a large church. You would think this person must be trustworthy; after all he was a trusted church leader. Unfortunately, their trust was misplaced. The senior pastor of the church lost $400,000. Other staff members lost sums in the tens of thousands. As to family members, some lost millions. In the end, north of $3 million disappeared and the advisor went to jail for nearly three years.

This loss could have been avoided if people had asked a few questions and did a little checking. If they had, they would have learned the guy was not registered or licensed with any regulatory agency but was charging a fee. Clearly illegal.

That's a deal breaker right there. None of these people had management agreements in place, and he certainly didn't acknowledge he was a fiduciary. He sold to the emotion of greed, suggesting he had the ability to get high rates of return trading options.

You might be saying to yourself, well, they were just plain stupid. But people can do stupid things. I'm reminded of an armed robbery at a convenience store I once investigated. The clerk working the midnight shift was held up at knife point. He opened the cash drawer and handed over the cash.

The offender then pulled out his wallet, grabbed his driver's license, laid it on the counter and said, "If the police want to know who did this, here's my ID."

When I was assigned the case for follow up, I thought nobody's that stupid; this must be a lost or stolen driver's license. Wrong. It was the guy. When I found him, he admitted to it and was charged with armed robbery.

This is probably too blunt, but an investor shouldn't be as stupid as this guy. Don't be stupid or lazy; do some investigation. I would highly recommend following the advice of President Ronald Reagan: "Trust but verify."

## Experience and Credentials

Working with advisors who have lots of experience or specialized training is beneficial, but advisors with advanced training aren't always better than advisors without it. My preference is to place a greater weight on experience.

In basic training as a policeman, we learned how to arrest a suspect: how to do a search and pat down, proper handcuffing procedures—these sorts of things. It always started with, "Put your hands on the wall." The instructor would do so. We would pat him down. He usually had a gun hidden somewhere we had to find before going through the handcuffing.

But what happens when you get on the street and you tell

the suspect, "Put your hands on the wall," and he looks at you and says, "No." I only had one guy resist arrest. He had placed his hands on the wall but then he took off running. Back then I was a young flat belly and I could run pretty good myself. The guy made it about fifteen yards before I tackled him.

> **We learn by doing, which includes making mistakes and figuring out how to fix them.**

He learned something that day and so did I.

There's a difference between basic training and street smarts. And that's true for any career: police officer, plumber, mechanic, financial advisor. We learn by doing, which includes making mistakes and figuring out how to fix them.

Finding an advisor does not need to be a laborious job. Some reliable internet sites are very useful and trustworthy.

*Dave Ramsey Solutions*: Dave Ramsey is an author who hosts the third largest radio talk show in America. *The Dave Ramsey Show* is heard by more than fourteen million listeners each week on more than six hundred stations, *The Dave Ramsey Show* podcast, SiriusXM, iHeartRadio, and a 24-hour online streaming video channel. The caller-driven show features Ramsey's advice on avoiding money mistakes and his step-by-step plan to get them out of debt.

*The Dave Ramsey Show* celebrated twenty-five years on the air in 2017. Ramsey Solutions uses common sense education to empower people to win at life and money. Through the Ramsey Solutions SmartVestor program you can find qualified Investing professionals near you that have been vetted by Ramsey Solutions.

*The Certified Financial Planner Board* has made finding a Certified Financial Planner (CFP®) professional simple. These professionals are rigorously trained in seventy-two areas of financial expertise and must accrue thousands of hours of experience prior to earning their certification. These planners are required to sign a code of ethics and complete continuing education requirements.

With a CFP® professional, you get a financial partner committed to working in your best interest and the confidence that comes with building a comprehensive plan. More information can be found at www.letsmakeaplan.org.

*BrokerCheck* is a free tool to research the background and experience of financial brokers, advisors, and advisory firms. It helps you make informed choices about brokers and brokerage firms by providing easy access to investment advisor information. You can search for a specific advisor or advisory firm by zip code. Screens by zip code can be further refined by asking for those that are investment advisors, brokers, or both. You can also set a distance you are willing to travel from that zip code. Their website is www.brokercheck.finra.org.

Finding a smart, ethical, and trustworthy advisor is important. But it's also helpful to understand the various costs associated with the variety of investment products they will show you. They're in a document called a prospectus, but who reads those? The next chapter goes into that often confusing subject.

## TAKEAWAYS

- Trustworthy advisors aren't selling returns or high-commission products. They are fiduciaries selling a service for a fee.
- Follow the advice of President Ronald Reagan when choosing a financial advisor, even if he is family or a friend: "Trust but verify."
- Use free internet sites like the Certified Financial Planner Board and BrokerCheck to vet potential advisors.

# 6

## Counting the Costs
## Returns Aren't Everything

Investors tend to focus on performance when it comes to choosing a financial advisor, but returns aren't everything. What's important is whether you make what you need. That's an absolute number. If you need (or desire) $20,000 a year from your investments and your advisor achieves that, I would say he's successful. Good results for the last five years by a fund manager doesn't necessarily equate to good results for the next five years. A better indicator of success is cost.

Understanding the costs associated with various investment vehicles is critical. Morningstar, Inc., a global financial services firm headquartered in Chicago, provides an array of independent investment research. In 2016 they conducted a study of mutual funds to identify what criteria have the greatest predictive power for future success or failure as it relates to a fund's returns. If you think it's past performance or manager tenure, you would be mistaken. Morningstar's research shows that the funds with the lowest cost (expense ratio) had the greatest likelihood of future success.

One of the big advantages of working with an advisor is

> **Morningstar's research shows that the funds with the lowest cost (expense ratio) had the greatest likelihood of future success.**

that he or she will evaluate the costs of investment vehicles and will make a recommendation or decision (if they have the discretion) as to which funds should be considered for a portfolio. Let's look at three types of professionally managed investment vehicles commonly considered by an investor or investment advisor and count their costs.

## Costs of Annuities

I usually say annuities are a bad idea because they are the most expensive. They are least attractive when you're in the accumulation phase of your financial journey. When you're in the disbursement phase, depending on your circumstances, an annuity may make sense. The traditional annuity has a lot of things in the contract that are not advantageous to the investor. These are higher costs, limited investment options, and contractual restrictions that affect liquidity.

When it comes to costs, traditional annuities have mortality, administrative, and subaccount expense charges.

The mortality charge is typically about 1.25 percent. Now, an annuity is not an investment. It is an investment *vehicle*. The actual investment inside an annuity is called a subaccount.

Subaccounts have additional expenses that are called expense ratios. These fees can be hefty and range from 0.6 percent to 1.25 percent. Most annuities carry a total annual cost of 2.5 percent. These expenses are charged over the life of the contract and never go away. So how does this cost affect your returns?

Imagine you invest $25,000 today in an actively managed mutual fund, leave it invested for thirty years, and earn 8 percent annually (net of expenses). It would grow to about $251,566. Now, invest those same dollars in an annuity and receive a 5.5 percent return (8 percent minus expenses of 2.5 percent). It would grow to just $124,598. That's about an $126,968 difference!

Investors don't realize how much more money they could earn with the same size investment because the advisor doesn't tell them. As I said before, some advisors sell to fear: "By investing in this annuity you will never lose your original investment. It's safe!"

But that protection is costly. And as I also pointed out, historically you only have about a 2 percent chance of losing your money over a long investment time horizon. Time mitigates risk and costs have a significant impact on results.

That covers the cost, but there are liquidity issues to consider as well. Traditional annuities also contractually obligate the contract owner to pay surrender charges if they surrender their annuity too soon. Typically these surrender charges apply for seven years and start at 7 percent and then go down by 1 percent for each year you hold the contract. Some contracts have surrender charges as high as 15 percent and don't go away for fifteen years.

While working with a client on his financial plan, I came

across an annuity contract he was sold. Sure enough, there was a fifteen-year surrender charge on the contract. If that wasn't bad enough, he was seventy years old when he made the purchase. He will be eighty-five years old before he can get 100 percent of his money without surrender. Of course, he could take up to 10 percent of the contract value annually with no surrender charge. Probably not much help if he ever became ill and needed to cover healthcare expenses.

Imagine you are home one afternoon and someone tries to break into your house. You immediately call 911 and are told an officer will be out next week. Doesn't help much, does it? And neither do annuities when you need money now and you must pay a penalty to get it. Maybe even a fifteen-year penalty!

Well, why the surrender charge? The short answer is the agent selling the annuity gets paid a commission on the products he sells. The commission can be healthy; as high as 7, 8, even 10 percent. A $100,000 annuity with a 7 percent commission pays $7,000. That's a pretty good day at the office. The insurance company amortizes those commission expenses over the seven-year surrender period of the contract.

But guess what? After seven years if you continue to hold the annuity, the insurance company does not reduce the expenses of the contract.

Annuities that are funded with pretax deposits or premiums are called qualified contracts. Insurance industry advisors often recommend annuities for IRAs. Why? An IRA opened with a brokerage firm has the same tax advantage as a qualified annuity without all the additional costs. Frankly there is no additional tax advantage. Maybe it has something to do with the healthy commissions. Or am I just being cynical? Guess that's the cop in me, always looking for motive.

Annuities can also be issued on a nonqualified basis. Nonqualified contracts also provide tax deferred growth. These contracts are funded with after-tax contributions and can be advantageous for very wealthy investors who want to defer tax to a later date when they may be in a lower tax bracket. When you keep Uncle Sam out of your pocket, you keep more of your money and it keeps growing.

If an investor currently owns a nonqualified annuity and there's no more surrender charge, it can make sense to transfer to a new annuity contract. This is called a 1035 exchange and is not a taxable event. I recommend doing this, but only if the new contract has significantly lower costs. Available in the marketplace today are annuity contracts with administrative costs as low as 0.25 percent, provide no death benefit, have subaccount fees far less than 1 percent, and never have a surrender charge. I often refer to these as no-load contracts.

The cost difference between the traditional annuity and no-load annuity can be as much as 1.5 percent. Unfortunately, insurance advisors often recommend transferring qualified annuities to a new contract or recommend a 1035 exchange for a nonqualified annuity as soon as surrender charges are gone. This is called "churning." But the second you do that, a new surrender period is started and the advisor gets another commission, unless it's a no-load contract.

## Costs of Mutual Funds

There are two breeds of mutual funds. One is commonly referred to as a load fund, the other as no-load. Load funds charge an upfront sales charge (a percentage of the investment) that's charged when you initially invest in the funds, or they charge a redemption fee, or contingent deferred sales charge, that's assessed for some period after every initial purchase.

Load funds are differentiated by a naming convention of share class. These share classes are class A, B, or C. Also available are institutional share class funds that do not charge an upfront sales charge or have deferred sales charges. These are commonly referred to as no-load funds.

All load and no-load funds carry an additional charge called an expense ratio. You don't see it in dollars; it's usually a percentage assessed against the mutual fund's net asset value daily. The total expense ratio may also include a fee called a 12b-1, which is a service fee or distribution fee. In either case, the 12b-1 fee is normally paid to compensate people who are selling the fund. The higher the fee, the more incentive there is for them to recommend it.

| SHARE CLASSES FOR INDIVIDUAL INVESTORS | | | | |
|---|---|---|---|---|
| SHARE CLASSES | FRONT-END LOAD | BACK-END LOAD | 12b-1 FEES | OTHER ANNUAL EXPENSES |
| CLASS A SHARES | Initial sales charge | NONE | Lower than B & C shares | Lower than B & C shares |
| CLASS B SHARES | NONE | Declines over a few years | Higher than A shares | Between A and C shares |
| CLASS C SHARES | If charged, lower than Class A | Usually lower than Class B and only charged for 1 year | Higher than A shares | Highest |
| Institutional Shares | NONE | NONE | LOWEST | LOWEST |

Let's say the total expense ratio of a mutual fund is 0.75 percent; 0.50 percent goes the asset management firm for the day-to-day management of the fund. The remaining 0.25 percent goes to the broker of record. This is one of the ways a broker gets paid.

You'll never get away from asset-management fees, but you

could avoid the ongoing 12b-1 fees by buying no-load funds or institutional share class funds. A broker who is working for commissions and not for a fee will sell you A, B, or C shares because his firm is paid an upfront sales charge and gets the 12b-1 fee in perpetuity.

## Costs of Exchange-Traded Funds

An exchange-traded fund (ETF) is a basket of stocks like a mutual fund that trades in real time, unlike a mutual fund that's bought and sold based on the end-of-the-day closing price or net asset value (NAV). Typically, an ETF is not actively managed by a portfolio manager who is making security selection decisions, but is passive and replicates some part of the market.

The expense ratios on ETFs are much lower than on mutual funds. ETFs do not charge a 12b-1 fee. The management fees on ETFs can range from as low as 0.04 percent for a broad-market large-company fund to 0.15 percent or 15 basis points for sector and domestic small-company funds. This is far lower than the management fee of 0.50 percent to 1 percent charged by mutual fund companies.

ETFs are highly liquid instruments and usually do not pay long-term capital gains. This provides for a tax advantage until the shares are sold. Today you can invest in an ETF that's invested in very specific segments of the market, like any of the eleven sectors of the S&P 500. For example, a healthcare sector fund holds a diversified portfolio of just healthcare stocks, or a financials sector fund holds just financial stocks. Some ETFs go further and focus on industries within a sector. For example, within the healthcare sector you could hold companies in the medical devices space or just biotech stocks.

Other investable ETFs include broad-market domestic equities, fixed-income securities, broad-market international securities, or those that invest in a specific region or country.

Finally, there are rules-based ETFs. The securities held in these ETFs are determined with the application of specific rules. For example, portfolios of

- low-volatility stocks: stocks that are less volatile than the broad market;
- value stocks: stocks trading at a price lower than their intrinsic value;
- quality stocks: stocks of large companies with a long history of paying their dividends;
- momentum stocks: stocks whose price is trending higher.

Keep in mind that the expense ratios of ETFs will vary like mutual funds but are often less expensive due to their passive nature.

In general, the insurance advisor will recommend annuities, while the broker advisor will recommend some load-share class. The registered investment advisor will typically recommend an institutional-share class mutual fund or an ETF. These instruments all vary in cost and may come with a range of penalties. To use the terminology from my old job, I would say the costs and penalties with annuities are in the felony class, load funds are in the misdemeanor class, and institutional mutual funds or ETFs are in the petty offense class.

As an investor, you have to know who you are dealing with, what they are selling and why, and how much you stand to gain or lose by following their advice. It's your money and it's your responsibility in any sales transaction to remember: *caveat emptor,* "let the buyer beware."

So, when should you use a financial advisor? The answer is always. Investment products are very sophisticated, with new products coming online all the time. Unless you do this every day and you know what to look for, you can quickly wind up in the weeds.

Is there anybody looking out for your financial best interest? If you think the government or Wall Street is on your side, think again, as you will learn in the next chapter.

## TAKEAWAYS

- Research shows that the funds with the lowest cost (expense ratio) have the greatest likelihood of future success.
- Costs matter a lot. Make sure you understand all the costs and be a smart consumer.
- When should you use a financial advisor? The answer is always. Investment products are very sophisticated, with new products coming online all the time.

# 7

# Government and Wall Street
# Not There for Everyone

Ronald Regan once said, "The most terrifying words in the English language are: 'I'm from the government and I'm here to help.'"

I used to say something like that, too.

"Hi, I'm Detective Wall and I'm here to help."

Well, that may be true, but not always. I guess it depends whether I was talking to the victim or the suspect.

## Government

If you think the US government always has your best interests at heart or is there to protect the investor, you are sadly mistaken. Sure, the government spends billions of dollars funding numerous regulatory agencies to provide oversight of the banks, insurers, brokers, and investment advisors. And yes, enforcement actions have been taken against these groups, and there are many conscientious civil servants who are trying to stop the bad guys. But if you have enough clout, (read "money"), and know the right people (read "politicians"), the rules often don't seem to apply and laws appear to be broken with impunity. This is likely not new information if you are familiar with recent history.

The government should be there to protect the investor and prevent fraud. One way they do this is through the SEC— Securities and Exchange Commission. Their website says,

"The mission of the US Securities and Exchange Commission is to protect investors, maintain fair, orderly, and efficient markets, and facilitate capital formation."

There are good things the SEC does, but they're over-worked. As an examiner once told me, "There's a lot more of you than there are of us." The SEC has made an effort to bring greater transparency to costs and expenses. One way they've done that is in going after the prospectus on mutual funds to show what the internal costs would be for a $100 investment for one year, three years, and five years. It's no longer buried way back on page 40 of the prospectus; rather it's there in the first few pages in an effort to be more transparent about costs.

> The love of money can be the root of all kinds of evil. The 2008 meltdown is just one example.

This action was helpful but the SEC has often failed to protect investors. Many have been defrauded by the Bernie Madoffs of the world or big players on Wall Street.

## Wall Street

Wall Street is a street in New York City where the Stock Exchange and financial businesses are located. It's the hub of the financial world and the historic headquarters of some of the largest US brokerages and investment banks like Goldman Sachs, Morgan Stanley, and J. P. Morgan Chase. It's also the place where individual investors can get involved in the financial markets through the purchase of stocks, bonds, and other financial instruments.

Wall Street is controlled by what I call "the boys in the club." Sometimes they lose their direction and become more interested in profits, with little regard for the everyday investor. And when things go south, they seldom take responsibility for their actions. They are an arrogant lot. Money seems to do that to people. Money is not evil, but the love of money is the root of all kinds of evil. The 2008 meltdown is just one example.

The Financial Crises Inquiry Committee completed their study on the 2008 financial crisis in 2011, but the study wasn't made public for five years. That's when we learned there were eleven referrals to the US Attorney General's office for possible prosecution. Now, you may be thinking the report was sealed to cover up the alleged crimes of the offenders. Being a skeptic, I think that may be partially true. When I investigated serious crimes, I often needed to do so with some secrecy. A secret investigation may have been the motive here, but as you will learn later in this chapter, that wasn't the case.

By that time, about four million families had lost their homes to foreclosure. Another 4.5 million families had slipped into the foreclosure process or were seriously behind in their mortgage payments. Nearly $11 trillion in household wealth had vanished, with retirement accounts and life savings swept away.

Many financial industry experts and top public officials were interviewed. Some testified that they were blindsided by the crisis and described it as a dramatic turn of events. Even those who worried the housing bubble might burst did not expect the magnitude of the crisis that would ensue. Charles Prince, the former chairman and chief executive officer of Citigroup Inc., called the collapse in housing prices wholly unanticipated.

That's an interesting perspective. Richard Bowen was a former business chief underwriter at Citigroup during the financial meltdown. He saw firsthand the fraud inside the organization. He was the Citigroup whistleblower who repeatedly warned Citi executive management about risky business practices and potential losses related to mortgage lending. He discovered that as many as 60 percent of the loans Citi was buying were defective.

Bowen alerted his top managers, who did nothing about it. He finally took his warnings to the Chairman of the Board,

Robert Rubin, the former US Treasury Secretary during the Clinton Administration. Bowen was subsequently demoted and placed on administrative leave. He subsequently reported his findings to the SEC where he provided a thousand pages of evidence of fraudulent activities prior to the bank bailouts.

People at the highest levels of Wall Street were not watching out for the investor. They were more concerned with selling mortgages and making more money. The thing about it is that they weren't left holding the bag. They sold those mortgages to Fannie Mae and Freddie Mac. These are quasi-government organizations that fund most of the mortgages for private homes in the US. This means that taxpayers basically fund these institutions.

Then the private insurers like AIG got in trouble because they insured this stuff without looking at any of the investments in the portfolios.

Neither the public mortgage companies or private insurance companies did their due diligence and it was the US taxpayers who suffered because of it.

## Collateral Consequences

In 2009, Congress and the White House created the Financial Crisis Inquiry Commission to investigate the causes of the financial crisis. According to chairman Phil Angelides, the commission sent eleven separate criminal referrals. These were recommendations to investigate or prosecute multiple high-level executives and companies to the Justice Department. He said, "It was one of the very disappointing legacies of the financial crisis. The simple fact is the Department of Justice never mobilized the resources to thoroughly investigate the wrongdoing that occurred in the run-up to the financial crisis. ... It remains an enigma to me."

Ten years earlier, Eric Holder, who was deputy attorney general in the Clinton administration and who later became US

Attorney General in 2008 during the Obama administration, wrote a memorandum titled "Bringing Criminal Charges Against Corporations." The memo states that prosecutors should take "collateral consequences" into account when conducting an investigation, determining whether to bring charges, and negotiating plea agreements. Hmmm, seems like maybe a lot of collateral consequences here, like eleven million hard-working Americans. Oh, that's right, they weren't "corporations." But in 2016, Holder told CNN, "We simply didn't have the proof. If we could've made those cases, we certainly would've brought them."

No proof!

Paul Pelletier, former senior prosecutor in the US Justice Department Criminal Division's Fraud Section became frustrated by lack of action and resigned. When he left the Justice Department he said high-level executives weren't prosecuted because of a lack of commitment, competence, and courage by the political leaders in the Department of Justice.

In July 2008, long after the risky, nontraditional mortgage market disappeared and the Wall Street mortgage securitization machine ground to a halt, the Federal Reserve adopted new rules to curb the abuses about which consumer groups raised red flags for years. But the damage was done. The total value of mortgage-backed securities issued between 2001 and 2006 reached $13.4 trillion.

The financial debacle was the result of three things: greedy Wall Street firms ignoring the warning signs of disaster; clueless politicians saying everybody should own a house; and shortsighted consumers borrowing money they knew they had no ability to repay.

The landscape hasn't really changed since 2008. When it comes to the government and Wall Street, just remember, they don't protect the everyday investor. That should be the role of the financial advisor, so it's important you chose the right one. So much for the government. Let's move on to the media and advertising.

## TAKEAWAYS

- The SEC's mission is to protect investors, maintain fair and efficient markets, and facilitate capital formation, but they're overworked and can't always do this.
- Wall Street is controlled by "the boys in the club" who are sometimes more interested in profits and have little regard for the everyday investor.
- The 2008 financial debacle was the result of three things: greedy Wall Street firms, clueless politicians saying everybody should own a house; and shortsighted consumers borrowing money they couldn't repay.

# 8

# Media and Advertising
# Selling to Fear and Greed

I place media in two broad categories. In the first are the advertisers who sell products by appealing to two emotions: fear and greed. They use celebrity endorsements, which are a very effective form of advertisement in social media, radio, and TV. It's easy to see how this would work in our celebrity-obsessed society. But does a celebrity endorsement really mean a product is superior to the competition? No. It simply means one company has a bigger marketing budget than the other guys do. Despite this, consumers still fall for this gimmick every day.

In the second category are the radio and TV business or market programs. These feature well-known personalities such as Suze Orman or Dave Ramsey. Many programs provide good, solid personal coaching.

Traditional media outlets offer programing that provides market commentary and interviews with leading current or former corporate executives. Professional money managers are also interviewed. Both are meant to be informative and objective, but can sometimes be prone to subjective analysis.

## Advertising
Every day I see financial advisors selling to fear. It must work because those ads aren't cheap. They wouldn't keep running them if they didn't make money. When you see or hear ads for

financial products or services, ask yourself, what emotions are they appealing to?

One such advertisement is of the guy selling gold from the deck of the USS Iowa with a big cannon behind him. He's saying you have to buy gold to protect your investment. His message is the world's going into the toilet!

Now, I'm not really sure how owning gold actually protects my other investments. Stock and bond prices go down whether I own gold or not. There's all this gloom and doom; then they sell something in the end: "The world's in chaos, but call this 800 number and purchase an investment product (gold), or call for a free investment guide (if you have at least $500,000 to invest)."

Okay, that's somebody selling to fear. That doesn't elicit trust from me.

I see a lot of these advertisers on news channels. For me, they are annoying. I feel like calling the networks and asking if they'll take the commercial off the air if I buy an ounce of gold. Likely not.

Advisors regularly promote vague or imprudent investment opportunities or services. For example, Fox News runs an ad where the so called "expert" tells us if silver goes back to its all-time high, you would have a return of 250 percent. He says if he could invest in just one thing, it would be silver. And I always scratch my head and think you can invest in just one thing. Nobody's stopping you. Go ahead, put all your money in silver. But why would you?

Consider this comparison. At one point, JCPenney traded at less than $1 a share. If you bought stock and it went to its all time high, you'd have more than a 4,000 percent gain. Of course, the company is in debt to the tune of about $1 billion and is closing stores. And there's this competitor called Amazon. But somehow the guy promoting silver doesn't connect those same dots for silver as to why it's priced the way it is.

You can't avoid media and advertising, but you can be discerning about what you see and hear. Listen for the motivation behind the message.

## Media

With the advent of the twenty-four-hour news cycle, the mainstream media is full of chatter about the capital markets. That chatter can be hazardous to your financial health. Every day the talking heads must give an explanation of why the markets went up or down. Some of it is valid, and I will listen to the information if it makes sense.

**The constant barrage from the media can affect us emotionally, often resulting in euphoria or panic.**

The recent coronavirus event is one example. It disrupted supply chains and corporate earnings. This created a lot of uncertainty resulting in extreme volatility. If there's one thing the markets detest, it's uncertainty. So this event, at least in the short term, explained the behavior of the markets. But at other times the reason may be as simple as there were more buyers or sellers on a particular day.

The constant barrage from the media can affect us emotionally, often resulting in euphoria or panic. Lead stories or headlines are often about how much the market was up or down. When it is down they say things like, "Today's drop was the largest since [a certain day, month, or year]." It doesn't matter what time period they pick; you can bet it's bad news. We likely think of selling on this news, but we probably should not.

When it's bad news, or really bad news, your emotion of fear is triggered and you are tempted to make irrational decisions. That's when we should be buying, but most investors get scared and sell. That's what I call "stinkin' thinkin'."

In March 2020 when the market dropped more than 30 percent, we received a call from a client. She was petrified. No talking her off the ledge. She told us to sell everything. The consequences—more than $50,000 in realized losses. Of course the market corrected, and she missed one of the fastest, sharpest rebounds in history.

Consider the following when those dark clouds arise:

- If I sell my stocks now, what's my plan for getting back in?
- Has my time horizon, risk profile, or circumstances meaningfully changed enough to warrant a portfolio change?
- Will my lifestyle be impacted in a meaningful way if stocks continue to fall?
- Did I build my portfolio with the understanding that stocks can and will fall on occasion?
- Have I overestimated my appetite for risk assets?
- Do I need to use the money I have invested in stocks for spending purposes in the next three to five years?
- Does my portfolio match my willingness, need, and ability to take risk?
- Do I fully understand the potential range of outcomes when investing in stocks?
- Is my portfolio durable and diversified enough to withstand severe dislocations in the stock market?
- Does my investment strategy fit with my personality?
- How did I react to market carnage in the past?
- How much volatility am I willing to accept in order to earn higher returns over time?
- What are my core investment beliefs?
- What do I own and why do I own it?
- What will cause me to buy or sell securities, funds, or asset classes in my portfolio?

There are no right or wrong answers to these questions, just personal answers. These questions are valid in every market environment, but more so when volatility rears its ugly head. We want to take the wheel to make something happen. It gives us the illusion of control. Until you sell, you haven't lost anything.

Most of this stuff boils down to having realistic expectations and a comprehensive investment plan in place to guide your actions. My suggestion is to ignore the advertisers and the media. Work with a competent advisor who has your best interests at heart and is trained to take the wheel when the road ahead is uncertain.

## TAKEAWAYS

- Advertisers who sell products often appeal to two emotions: fear and greed.
- Every day the talking heads must give an explanation of why the markets went up or down. But the reason may be as simple as there were more buyers or sellers on a particular day.
- A good plan to deal with stock volatility is to have realistic expectations and a comprehensive investment plan in place to guide your actions.

# 9

# Investment Disciplines
# Portfolio Management

This is a nuts-and-bolts chapter. It gets into the various investment pieces—cash, bonds, stocks, and real estate— and some of the complexities of these investments. We will look at how advisors build portfolios and keep them running. Some build for speed, which involves greater risk. Others are after endurance and build for the long haul. This peek under the hood behind the garage door will help you better understand what financial advisors do and help you decide which approach is the best fit for you.

Some of you may be do-it-yourselfers when it comes to investments. I can identify. Years ago I used to work on my own cars. One time I repaired my car by replacing the choke pull-off. The engine still ran poorly, though, so I took it to a local mechanic. When I picked it up, the guy asked me one question:

"Who installed the choke pull-off?"

I reluctantly admitted I had.

He had three words for me, "It was backwards."

That was last my attempt to fix my car. Since then, automobiles have only become more complex. This is why I depend on professional mechanics to keep my car running.

Registered investment advisors are trained professionals. They provide two valuable services: financial planning and wealth management. Some just do financial planning while others offer both services. In this chapter, I'll focus on wealth-management services.

## Management Discipline

Some advisors take a strategic approach allocating the portfolio across various asset classes such as cash, bonds, stocks, and real estate. They set target weights for each broad asset class, with an occasional rebalance back to the target. Other advisors are more active, dynamically managing the broad asset class mix and/or securities held in a portfolio.

Advisors with a dynamic approach means they actively trade shifting toward the segment of the market they believe is more attractive. This results in more buying and selling of positions resulting in higher turnover in the portfolio.

An investment portfolio can be built with mutual funds or exchange-traded funds (ETFs). These instruments are baskets of stocks or a pooled portfolio of securities that have similar characteristics—for example, big company stocks like Walmart and Walgreens, or small company stocks like Texas Roadhouse. Most small company stocks are not household names and are more likely to be companies you've never heard of.

Another approach is to manage portfolios of individual stocks and bonds. Still others will hold individual positions as well as mutual funds and ETFs.

It is important for investors to understand how the advisor identifies which types of securities will be held in the portfolio. Some advisors manage on a discretionary basis. This allows them to buy and sell securities in a portfolio without notifying or getting approval from the client. Others serve in a nondiscretionary role. They will speak to their client and recommend the sale or purchase of a security before executing the transaction.

Let's take a little deeper dive into each of these approaches. Warning, this may be a little technical. You will likely come across some terminology you may not be familiar with. If so, refer to the glossary at the back of the book.

## Asset Classes

When it comes to the asset classes mentioned above, cash is the safest place to invest and produces the lowest returns. Cash includes instruments that can be quickly sold without the loss of any principal—things like savings accounts and money markets.

Bonds are the next safest asset class and produce returns greater than cash but less than equities. Bonds are loans. An investor agrees to lend money for a fixed rate of return, called coupons or the interest rate. The prices of bonds can change as interest rates change. When interest rates go up, bond prices go down. When interest rates go down, bond prices go up. Inflation is one variable that produces higher interest rates. This requires a higher rate of return thereby decreasing a bond's price. The longer the maturity, the lower the coupon; and the lower the quality, the more volatile the price. Issuers of bonds can be governments (domestic and foreign), corporations, and municipalities, which may provide tax-free income.

Equities (stocks) generally produce the greatest returns over a long holding period. This is because equities are ownership. Would you rather own property and collect rent or be a tenant and pay rent? Most agree, owning is better because the tenant pays rent. This provides income that the owner can use to pay the expenses of owning the building. If the rental income is greater than the expenses, the owner puts the rest in his pocket. But the owner gets one more benefit: appreciation, or the value of the building going up over time. Of course, owning comes with additional risk. Sometimes tenants don't pay the rent or damage the property, resulting in costly repairs.

Like the landlord, owning the common stock (equities) of

companies puts you in the position of ownership with many other investors.

The last asset class is real estate, which can be owned in two forms. You are most likely familiar with private real estate such as land, apartments, malls, industrial buildings, or single family residences. However, investing in private real estate requires large sums of cash and is not very liquid. Most investors do not have the capital necessary to buy buildings or land.

Real estate investment trusts (REITS) provide another mechanism for owning real estate. A REIT is a company owning and typically operating real estate that generates income. Properties in a REIT portfolio may include apartment complexes, data centers, healthcare facilities, hotels, infrastructure (fiber cables, cell towers, and energy pipelines), office buildings, retail centers, self-storage, timberland, and warehouses. REITS provide the investor a high degree of liquidity, a well-diversified portfolio of companies, and smaller initial investments because they are traded on our exchanges.

## Passive or Active

Now that you are familiar with the investable broad asset classes, let's look at how investors can invest in these segments of the market. The advisor can build a portfolio utilizing mutual funds or ETFs and typically constructs a well-diversified portfolio of stocks and bonds. It will likely include large-and-small company domestic stocks, international stocks, and REITs, as well as fixed-income or bond funds.

These instruments fall into two broad categories: passive or active. A passive fund merely holds a basket of securities that replicate or are a shadow of a segment of the capital markets. These segments are commonly called indices. The S&P 500 is one such index and consists of the 500 largest companies in the US. It is representative of more than 90 percent of all large US companies traded on the exchanges. Passive instruments are very inexpensive because there is no active component in their management. The returns of these funds will closely track the returns of the S&P 500.

An advisor could also choose to use an actively managed fund where a portfolio fund manager selects individual securities he believes will appreciate more than the broad market. These funds are more expensive because a manager actively engages in security selection.

Advisors who build portfolios with active funds will evaluate the fund objective and the management style of the fund. For example, does the fund own only big-company growth stocks, big-company value stocks, or a blend of the two? Growth stocks are considered stocks that have the potential to outperform the overall market over time because of their future potential. Value stocks are classified as stocks that are currently trading below what they are really worth and will, therefore, provide a superior return. Other criteria include performance results in the context of risks taken, performance relative to their peers, manager tenure, and costs.

**Quantitative or Qualitative**
Another approach is to build a portfolio of individual stocks. The advisors in this neighborhood may be trying to identify specific stocks with the objective of long-term growth with the goal of producing returns greater than the market. Or they may have a more conservative objective, to produce current income or own stocks with less risk as measured by variance of the stock's price known as standard deviation. These advisors will likely evaluate stocks based on fundamental quantitative or qualitative research.

The distinction between quantitative and qualitative approaches is like the difference between artificial intelligence and human intelligence. Quantitative analysis uses exact inputs such as profit margins, debt ratios, earnings multiples, and so on. These can be plugged into a computerized model to yield an exact result, such as the fair value of a stock or a forecast for earnings growth.

Of course, for the time being, a human must write the program that crunches these numbers. That involves a fair degree of subjective judgment. Once they are programmed, though, computers can perform quantitative analysis in nanoseconds that would take even the most gifted humans minutes or hours.

Qualitative analysis, on the other hand, deals with intangible, inexact concerns that belong to the social and experiential realm rather than the mathematical realm. This approach depends on the kind of intelligence that machines currently lack— things like positive associations with a brand, management trustworthiness, customer satisfaction, competitive advantage, and cultural shifts. These are difficult, if not impossible, to capture with numerical inputs.

## Managing Bonds

On the bond or fixed-income side, individual bonds can be purchased. Government bonds come in different flavors: US treasuries, agencies, mortgages, or municipal bonds, which may have tax benefits. Corporations also issue bonds. Some are of high quality, commonly called investment grade, which are less likely to default. Others are lower-quality bonds commonly called junk bonds. These are more likely to default (go out of business), but may offer greater returns. Advisors will construct portfolios of fixed-income securities with these types of bonds that will have different characteristics such as long or short maturities and different coupon or interest payment rates.

## Managing Market Sectors

Finally, the stock market is divided up into eleven sectors. One example is the healthcare sector. It consists of companies that produce healthcare products or provide healthcare services. Other sectors include financials, energy, utilities, and industrials.

Deep academic research has found that more value can be achieved by being in the right sector at the right time rather than owning the right company in a sector. Recently many new investment products that employ this strategy have been created and are available to investors. Deciding if you should choose to own Dell or HP is not the decision to make. When technology stocks are in favor, both Dell and HP should do well, so you could construct a portfolio that has a tilt to the technology sector as a whole.

Every year, on average, four sectors will have returns greater than the S&P 500. The difference between the best performing sector and the worst performing sector is often substantial. In 2008, a terrible year for the market, the S&P 500 returned

**Knowing *what not* to own is as important as knowing *what* to own.**

a negative 37 percent. The best-performing sector that year was consumer staples with a negative 15.4 percent return. The worst-performing sector was financials, checking in at a negative 55.3 percent. The difference between the best and worst was nearly 40 percent.

Knowing *what not* to own is as important as knowing *what* to own. More recently, in 2019, the best sector was technology, up 50.3 percent. The worst, energy, was up only 11.8 percent. The broad market, as represented by the S&P 500, was up 31.5 percent.

Selecting securities and building portfolios is not a simple task, just as I learned when it came to repairing automobile engines. New investment products are always coming to market that are more and more sophisticated. This is why everyday investors should use experienced advisors. Think experienced mechanics. That said, investors should understand the advisors' approach and advisors should be able to clearly communicate what they do and how they do it. If they can't, the investor should keep looking for someone who can.

The key to finding the right advisor is asking the right questions. I will give you some guidance in that area in the next chapter.

## TAKEAWAYS

- Registered investment advisors are trained professionals who provide two very important services: financial planning and wealth management.
- Research has found that more value can be achieved by being in the right sector at the right time rather than owning the right company in a sector.
- Knowing what not to own is as important as knowing what to own.

# 10

## The Interview
## Ask the Right Questions

We all rely on professionals, but not all professionals are competent. There are good mechanics and poor mechanics. There are good plumbers and poor plumbers. There are good financial advisors and poor financial advisors. Well, how do you find the good mechanics and plumbers and financial advisors? Here are three things to do:

- Check credentials
- Check references
- Ask the right questions

### Credentials

Credentials are important. They let you know what a person has been successfully trained to do. Typically, advisors put their credentials behind their names on their business cards or emails. In the financial services industry, a CFP® is the most prevalent. Those who have this credential are required to adhere to a strict code of ethics. They must have completed in-depth personal financial planning training, have several years of experience, and have passed a comprehensive exam. If there is a complaint made against a CFP®, the CFP® board can suspend or revoke their license. In short, they can be booted out of the business.

> Credentials are important. They let you know what a person has been successfully trained to do.

Another big one is a CPA, Certified Public Accountant. CPAs are usually the most trusted advisors. Many people go to CPAs to get their taxes done or to handle accounting for their business. Many CPAs have a securities license and broker-dealer relationship. Thus some CPAs may give investment advice. They will have passed a securities exam and can sell mutual funds. That does not mean they will provide thorough financial planning services.

Just to create a little more confusion here. Some CPA's have pursued and received a Personal Financial Specialist (PFS) credential. Those who have this credential must hold a valid CPA permit, license, or certificate issued by a state authority. Certification also requires many hours of on the job experience, formal personal financial planning training, and passing a personal financial planning exam.

A CPA is well trained but likely more proficient in one aspect of financial planning, such as tax planning and preparation. Most states have continuing education requirements for CPAs. A CFP® will have more broad-based training and experience in personal financial planning and wealth management. A CFP® also has continuing education requirements.

### References

Check the references of any financial advisor you are thinking about trusting with your financial future. Do you personally know anyone who has used them and would they recommend them? Will they let you talk to any of their customers without violating confidentiality?

Do they have any complaints against them? Go to https://brokercheck.finra.org/ and check on any advisor or brokerage firm you are considering using. The site will give you "a snapshot of a broker's employment history, regulatory actions, and investment-related licensing information, arbitrations and complaints."

The Financial Industry Regulatory Authority (FINRA) is a private, not-for-profit organization that oversees US broker-dealers. FINRA maintains websites where you can check out an advisor to see if there have been any complaints or findings made against an advisor. They publish a list of brokers they have barred at https://www.finra.org/rules-guidance/oversight-Oversight%20%26%20Enforcement/individuals-barred-finra.

The SEC Action Lookup tool (https://www.sec.gov/litigations/sec-action-look-up) lists formal actions the SEC has brought against individuals, including those who are not brokers.

The North American Securities Administrators Association (NASAA) maintains a list of state securities regulators (https://www.nasaa.org/contact-your-regulator/ who can provide additional research on brokers and investment advisors.

## The Right Questions

As a detective I had to determine if a crime had taken place. Then I had to identify the person responsible for the offense. In some cases, my job was to help clear the innocent. To do all this, I learned to ask victims and suspects the right questions. These centered on who, what, when, where, why, and how: Who had opportunity? What might someone's motive be? Where were they at the time of the incident?

The same is true for investors who are seeking to hire financial advisors. You need to ask questions to determine if the advisor has your best interests at heart, is just trying to sell you something, or perhaps even trying to swindle you. Here are some key questions to ask any advisor being considered for the job of managing your money.

**1. Are you a fiduciary?** (Remember, fiduciaries are required by law to place the clients' interests ahead of their own.)

If the answer to this question is no, there's no need to proceed with any other questions. The interview is over—just like when a suspect exercises his right to remain silent and asks to speak to a lawyer.

**2. Does your firm carry fiduciary liability insurance?**

This insurance is important because if there's a trade error and it's a large investment, somebody's going to pay—either the advisor or their insurance carrier.

**3. How long has your firm been in business?**

The longer the better. You don't want to be among the firm's first account, or an advisor's first account.

**4. How much time do you spend annually on continuing education or certification renewals?**

A good answer is ten to fifteen hours. A CFP® is required to complete thirty hours of continuing education every two years. Two of those hours must be training in ethics.

**5. What products and services does your firm offer? Are recommendations of products and services limited?**

If their recommendations of products and services are limited, that tells you he's a captive agent.

**6. What is your firm's investment philosophy? What are your strategies and disciplines? Are all of your accounts managed the same?**

Review chapter nine, which discusses this topic in greater detail.

**7. Is your firm compliant with the Global Investments Performance Standards (GIPS)? If not, why not?**

Be careful here. They may say the firm calculates returns

by this standard, but the firm itself is not compliant. They may be cherry-picking and showing you the returns of their best-performing account, or returns from a model and not an actual composite of accounts. This is misleading at best, or borderline fraud at worst.

**8. Can you provide a copy of the disclosure registration documents you have filed with the SEC?**

A registered investment advisor is required by law to give these documents to the prospective client before he becomes a client. So does a broker advisor, if he's charging a hard dollar fee. An insurance advisor doesn't have to do this.

**9. Have you or your firm been disciplined by any government regulator or professional organization for unethical or improper conduct? Has your firm ever filed a claim with an insurance carrier for breach of fiduciary duties?**

If a firm or advisor breached their fiduciary duty and was sued, they might file a claim with their fiduciary insurance carrier. If that happens in the institutional world, that firm or advisor is toast. I would strongly discourage an investor from working with that firm.

**10. How are you paid and how much are you paid? Do you make more money if I purchase a certain stock or security over another? Are you paid bonuses to recommend certain investments? Does your firm hold prize contests for sales?**

Be specific and ask, "If I invest $10,000 with you, how much will your firm be paid?"

**11. What other services does your fee cover? Financial planning? Estate planning? Budgeting advice?**

You want to know what the fees are going to cover. Is there an extra cost for things like a written financial plan, drawing up a trust, or preparing legal documents? Some advisors have an *a la carte* system where you pay for services as needed.

### 12. How often will we meet and how often will I receive reports about my portfolio?

I recommend quarterly reports and at least an annual face-to-face meeting. An advisor should always be available for a call and willing to meet if there's been a change in life circumstances, such as the loss of a job or death of a spouse. You want an advisor who's aware and responsive to your needs.

### 13. Do you and your firm's staff invest their personal assets like you invest your clients' assets? In other words, do you and your staff "eat your own cooking"?

If the answer is no, ask why not. Don't they believe in their own strategies and disciplines?

There's something else I learned in police work that also applies to interviewing potential financial advisors. When a suspect repeats the question I asked, he or she is getting ready to lie. If I ask, "What's your name?" and he says, "What's my name?" he's likely repeating my question because he's trying to think of a bogus name to give me.

"So, how much do you charge?"

"How much do I charge? Well, I charge ..."

Use caution when the advisor repeats or hesitates to answer your questions.

Asking these questions and weighing the answers will go a long way in helping you identify the smart, ethical, and trustworthy advisor. Realistic advisor accountability and expectations are the keys to avoiding disappointment in the future.

## TAKEAWAYS

- Three things to do when selecting a financial advisor: Check credentials, check references, and ask the right questions.
- The first question to ask a potential financial advisor is "Are you a fiduciary?" If the answer is no, the interview is over.
- Realistic advisor accountability and expectations are the keys to avoiding disappointment in the future.

# Conclusion

You can borrow money for a house or a car. You can cover college costs with scholarships, grants, student loans, or imagine this, by getting a part-time job. But try walking into a bank and asking for a loan to cover your retirement. Not going to happen. We must prioritize our financial goals and, for most people, the number one goal is saving for a comfortable retirement.

If you're not there already, you may be one day. Statistics from the National Institute on Retirement Security show that almost forty million households have nothing saved for retirement. And for the households that do have money saved, the average amount is about $230,000. That may sound like a lot until you consider that the estimated average medical costs per couple are almost $200,000. That doesn't leave much to live on.

Social Security can definitely help, but it was never designed to be the sole means of support. Especially now that people live decades longer than they did when it was first set up. In 2016, the average Social Security monthly check was $1,354—about what a minimum wage job pays. Not a lot to live on, much less travel and do the things many retirees dream of.

This lack of financial preparation has come about for many reasons. We live in a culture of instant gratification. We want what the Joneses have, and we want it now! Easy credit helps us slip into debt, and servicing that debt reduces our ability to save. We don't have a written budget or financial plan. And as the saying goes, "If it's not written down it's not a plan." And then there's good ole procrastination. When we do start saving, it may be too late to build an adequate retirement nest egg.

Whether some or none of these things are true for you, it's never too late to get help. A trustworthy team can make the difference between ending poorly and ending well.

One of my favorite TV programs from the 1980s was *Hill Street Blues*. The veteran cop Sgt. Phil Esterhaus ended the introductory roll call at the start of each show with the words, "Let's be careful out there." That was good advice for his officers and that's good advice for all investors.

# Glossary

**1035 exchange**: A provision in the Internal Revenue Service code allowing for a tax-free transfer of an existing annuity contract, life insurance policy, long-term care product, or endowment for another one of like kind.

**401k, 457, 403b**: Employer-sponsored payroll-deduction retirement savings plans that employees can contribute to, which offer certain tax advantages.

**Annuity**: A contract between you and an insurance company in which you make a lump-sum payment or series of payments and, in return, receive regular disbursements, beginning either immediately or at some point in the future.

**Asset allocation**: An investment strategy that balances risk and reward by apportioning a portfolio's assets according to an individual's goals, risk tolerance, and investment horizon. The three main asset classes—equities, fixed-income, and cash and equivalents—have different levels of risk and return.

**Basis point**: One hundredth of one percent, used chiefly in expressing differences of interest rates.

**Best interest rule**: SEC rule that requires broker-dealers to only recommend financial products to their customers that are in their customers' best interests. They have to clearly identify any potential conflicts of interest and financial incentives the broker-dealer may have with those products.

**Bond:** A fixed-income instrument that represents a loan made by an investor to a borrower (typically corporate or governmental). A bond could be thought of as an IOU between the lender and borrower that includes the details of the loan and its payment.

**Broker-dealer advisor:** Someone who, in addition to making trades on behalf of the client, provides investment advice. The broker-dealer advisor receives a fee in addition to the commissions given for the actual trades.

**Captive agent:** A licensed insurance agent of a single insurer or fleet of insurers who is obliged to submit business only to that company, or give that company first refusal rights on a sale. A captive agent is paid by that one company either with a combination of salary and commissions or with just commissions.

**Certified Financial Planner** (CFP®): A professional certification designation for financial planners conferred by the Certified Financial Planner Board of Standards. To receive authorization to use the designation, the candidate must meet education, examination, experience, and ethics requirements, and pay an ongoing certification fee.

**Composite:** An aggregation of one or more portfolios managed according to a similar investment mandate, objective, or strategy. It is the primary vehicle for presenting performance to clients. A firm must include all actual, fee-paying, discretionary portfolios in at least one composite.

**Equity:** The value of the shares issued by a company. Typically referred to as shareholder equity, which represents the amount of money that would be returned to a company's shareholders if all of the assets were liquidated and all the company's debt was paid off.

**Exchange-traded fund (ETF):** An investment fund traded on stock exchanges. An ETF holds assets such as stocks, commodities, or bonds and generally operates with an arbitrage mechanism designed to keep it trading close to its net asset value, although deviations can occasionally occur.

**Expense ratio:** This measures how much of a fund's assets are used for administrative and other operating expenses. An expense ratio is determined by dividing a fund's operating expenses by the average dollar value of its assets under management (AUM).

**Fee-only advisor:** Registered investment advisors with a fiduciary responsibility to act in their clients' best interest. They do not accept any fees or compensation based on product sales. Fee-only advisors have fewer inherent conflicts of interest. They generally provide more comprehensive advice.

**Fiduciary:** A person or organization that acts on behalf of another person or persons to manage assets. Essentially, a fiduciary owes to that other entity the duties of good faith and trust. The highest legal duty of one party to another, being a fiduciary requires being bound ethically to act in the other's best interests.

**The Financial Industry Regulatory Authority, Inc. (FINRA):** A private corporation that acts as a self-regulatory organization. It is a non-governmental organization that regulates member brokerage firms and exchange markets. It's the largest independent regulator for all securities firms doing business in the US.

**Fixed-income investment:** A type of investment security that pays investors fixed-interest payments until its maturity date. At maturity, investors are repaid the principal amount they invested.

**Global Investments Performance Standards (GIPS):** A set of voluntary standards used by investment managers throughout the world to ensure the full disclosure and fair representation of their investment performance. The goal of the standards is to make it possible for investors to compare one firm's performance against that of another firm.

**Mutual fund:** A type of financial vehicle made up of a pool of money collected from many investors to invest in securities like stocks, bonds, money-market instruments, and other assets. Mutual funds give small or individual investors access to professionally managed portfolios.

**Nonqualified annuity:** Any annuity not used to fund a tax-advantaged retirement plan or IRA. Contributions to nonqualified annuities are made with after-tax dollars and premiums are not deductible from gross income for income-tax purposes.

**Qualified annuity:** A qualified annuity is a retirement savings plan that is funded with pretax dollars.

**Registered investment advisor (RIA):** A person or firm who advises clients on investments and manages their portfolios. RIAs have a fiduciary duty to their clients. They have a fundamental obligation to provide investment advice that always acts in their clients' best interests.

**Roth IRA:** A tax-advantaged retirement savings account that allows you to withdraw your savings tax free. The biggest difference between Roth IRAs and traditional IRAs is how they are taxed.

**Securities Exchange Commission (SEC):** An independent federal government agency responsible for protecting investors, maintaining fair and orderly functioning of the securities markets, and facilitating capital formation.

**Stock**: Also known as "shares" or "equity," stocks are a type of security that signifies proportionate ownership in the issuing corporation. This entitles the stockholder to that proportion of the corporation's assets and earnings. Stocks are bought and sold predominantly on stock exchanges.

**Surrender charge**: A fee levied on a life-insurance policyholder upon cancellation of their life insurance policy. The fee is used to cover the costs of keeping the insurance policy on the insurance provider's books.

**Wrap account**: An investment portfolio managed by a brokerage firm for a flat fee charged quarterly or annually. The fee is based on total assets under management and includes all administrative, commission, and management expenses.

Made in the USA
Columbia, SC
24 May 2020